CHINESE PROVERBS FROM OLDEN TIMES

PETER
PAUPER
PRESS

MOUNT VERNON, NEW YORK

NOTE

EVERYBODY uses proverbs unconsciously in daily speech, and a people's language expresses character and color by such use. Scholars say the Chinese have more proverbs, and use them more, than any other people. This is natural enough, for the deference formerly paid in China to ancestors and traditions would encourage use of the old folk-wisdom. Our pleasure in hearing these proverbs comes sometimes from the echo they carry of our own familiar phrases, sometimes from the echo of city, mountain, and valley life strange and far. The present English renderings are free; and often attempt, but cannot recapture, the true telescopic-telegraphic brevity of the originals.

PROVERBS
FROM
OLDEN
TIMES

SWIFTEST HORSE
CANNOT OVERTAKE
THE WORD ONCE SPOKEN

BEFORE YOU BEAT THE DOG
LEARN HIS MASTER'S NAME

WE ALL LIKE LAMB...
EACH HAS A DIFFERENT
WAY OF COOKING IT

EVEN YOUR
OWN TEN FINGERS
ARE UNEQUAL

HIDE YOUR OFFENDED
HEART...
KEEP YOUR VALUED FRIEND

YELLOW GOLD...
PLENTIFUL COMPARED TO
WHITE-HAIRED FRIENDS

HE WHO CARVES
THE BUDDHA
NEVER WORSHIPS HIM

PLEASURES ARE SHALLOW
SORROWS DEEP

WITH TRUE FRIENDS . . .
EVEN WATER
DRUNK TOGETHER
IS SWEET ENOUGH

MAYBE NOT SO FINE
BUT MY COUNTRY'S WINE

CLEAR CONSCIENCE
NEVER FEARS
MIDNIGHT KNOCKING

ILLNESS COMES IN
BY MOUTH . . .
ILLS COME OUT BY IT

HONEST JUDGE
LEAN CLERKS...
POWERFUL GOD
FAT PRIESTS

THE DAY YOUR HORSE DIES
AND YOUR MONEY'S LOST...
YOUR RELATIVES
CHANGE TO STRANGERS

WHILE IT IS STILL
GOOD WEATHER...
CLEAN THE DRAINPIPES

IN A NARROW LANE
BEWARE ENEMIES

NEVER TRY TO CATCH
TWO FROGS
WITH ONE HAND

FISHES SEE THE WORM
NOT THE HOOK

WE FORGET EVEN INCENSE
IN EASY TIMES . . .
COME HARD TIMES
WE EMBRACE
THE BUDDHA'S FEET

FRIEND, DO NOT TRY
TO BORROW COMBS
FROM SHAVEN MONKS

FOOD CURES HUNGER
STUDY CURES IGNORANCE

THE CLEVER DOCTOR
NEVER TREATS HIMSELF

TWO GOOD TALKERS . . .
NOT WORTH
ONE GOOD LISTENER

MAN IS HEAVEN AND EARTH
IN LITTLE

ONE DOG
BARKS AT A SHADOW. . .
A HUNDRED
BARK AT HIS SOUND

EVEN IN A BAMBOO TUBE
SNAKES TRY TO WRIGGLE

CHANGE CLOTHES YOU CAN
YOU CANNOT
CHANGE THE MAN

AFTER GREAT THUNDER
LITTLE RAIN

TO MOVE A TREE
DIG UNDER THE ROOT

NO MELON-PEDDLER CRIES:
BITTER MELONS . . .
NO WINE-DEALER SAYS:
SOUR WINE

A NATION'S TREASURE...
SCHOLARS

DON'T WASTE GOOD IRON
FOR NAILS...
GOOD MEN FOR SOLDIERS

BITTER WORDS
ARE GOOD MEDICINE...
SWEET WORDS
CARRY INFECTION

TO TALK GOODNESS
IS NOT GOOD...
ONLY TO DO IT IS

ONE MAN TELLS A LIE...
DOZENS REPEAT IT
AS THE TRUTH

A GOOD NEIGHBOR...
A FOUND TREASURE

THE LITTLE LEARNED MAN
IS USEFUL TO THE STATE . . .
WHAT USE THE GREAT BIG
BLOCKHEAD?

NEW BOOTS: BIG STEPS

MALLET STRIKES CHISEL . . .
CHISEL SPLITS WOOD

EMPTY THE CLEAR PATH
TO HEAVEN . . .
CROWDED THE DARK ROAD
TO HELL

HONEST SCALES
AND FULL MEASURE
HURT NO MAN

IN ALL THE WORLD
PEOPLE ENJOY SALT
AND MONEY

EMPEROR'S RELATIVES TOO
WALK SOFTLY
IN STRAW SANDALS

FRIENDSHIPS LAST
AS LONG AS MEAT AND WINE;
MARRIAGES LAST
AS LONG AS RICE AND FUEL

IN MULTITUDES OF WORDS
SURELY SOME MISTAKES

THE GODS ... THOUSANDS
AND TEN THOUSANDS ...
ARE ONE GOD

IT'S YOUR OWN LANTERN ...
DON'T POKE HOLES
IN THE PAPER

BETTER LEAN AND GOOD
THAN FAT AND EVIL

THE RICH MAN PLANS
FOR TOMORROW...
THE POOR MAN FOR TODAY

WISE BEES SIP NOT
FROM FALLEN FLOWERS

MAN MUST BE SHARPENED
ON MAN
LIKE KNIFE ON STONE

FIREWOOD ALONE WILL NOT
START A FIRE

THE DOOR TO VIRTUE...
HEAVY AND HARD TO PUSH

DRAGON BEGETS DRAGON
PHOENIX BEGETS PHOENIX

EMPTY BOTTLE...
HOLLOW HOSPITALITY

THOUGH YOU HIDE IT
FROM MEN...
HEAVEN SEES YOUR ACT

SLANDER CANNOT DESTROY
AN HONEST MAN...
WHEN THE FLOOD RECEDES
THE ROCK IS THERE

EASY TO RUN DOWN HILL...
MUCH PUFFING TO RUN UP

THE BLIND
ARE QUICK TO HEAR...
THE DEAF TO SEE

NO NEEDLE IS SHARP
AT BOTH ENDS

DOCTORS WHO RIDE CHAIRS
NEVER RIDE THEM
TO HOVELS

HE WATCHES CHESS GAME
IN SILENCE...
WHAT A SUPERIOR MAN!

THE DRY FINGER
LIFTS NO SALT

THE YANGTSE
NEVER RUNS BACKWARD...
MAN RECAPTURES NOT
HIS YOUTH

GARDEN FLOWERS LARGER
FIELD FLOWERS STRONGER

IF YOU WANT YOUR DINNER
DON'T INSULT THE COOK

ABROAD
WE JUDGE THE DRESS...
AT HOME
WE JUDGE THE MAN

CONQUERORS ARE KINGS ...
THE BEATEN ARE BANDITS

A BAR OF IRON
CONTINUALLY GROUND ...
A NEEDLE

WORDS SPOKEN
MAY FLY AWAY ...
THE WRITING-BRUSH
LEAVES ITS MARK

WORK FEARS
THE BUSY MAN

SCHOOLMASTER
STICK TO YOUR BOOKS ...
FARMER, TO YOUR PIGS

BEFORE TELLING SECRETS
ON THE ROAD ...
LOOK IN THE BUSHES

GIRLS MARRY
TO PLEASE PARENTS...
WIDOWS
TO PLEASE THEMSELVES

HONEY IN HIS MOUTH
KNIVES IN HIS HEART

THAT MAN WHO KNOWS
TOO MANY TRADES...
HIS FAMILY STARVES

CURSE YOUR WIFE
AT EVENING...
SLEEP ALONE AT NIGHT

THE FULL TEAPOT
MAKES NO SOUND

WHEN WINGS ARE GROWN
BIRDS AND CHILDREN
FLY AWAY

TO BUILD IT, TOOK
ONE HUNDRED YEARS ...
TO DESTROY IT, ONE DAY

EASY TO KNOW MEN'S FACES
NOT THEIR HEARTS

ONE GENERATION PLANTS
THE TREES ...
ANOTHER GETS THE SHADE

FOR A SWIFT ARROW
PULL HARD ON THE STRING

NO MATTER HOW STOUT...
ONE BEAM
CANNOT SUPPORT A HOUSE

VIRTUOUS TEN YEARS
STILL NOT ENOUGH ...
EVIL ONE DAY
TOO MUCH ALREADY

MONEY WILL OPEN
BLIND MEN'S EYES ...
MONEY WILL CLOSE
FAT PRIESTS' EYES

GRASS FEARS THE FROST ...
FROST FEARS THE SUN

YOU CAN'T FILL YOUR BELLY
PAINTING PICTURES
OF BREAD

DON'T SEND A SMALL BOAT
FOR SUCH HEAVY CARGO

HE WHO WAS BITTEN
BY A SNAKE
AVOIDS TALL GRASS

DO NOT TEAR DOWN
THE EAST WALL
TO REPAIR THE WEST

SEEKING FISH?
DON'T DIVE IN THE POND...
GO HOME AND GET A NET

CLAY BUDDHA
SCORNS MUD BUDDHA

IF YOU SEEK A JEWEL
OF A WOMAN...
LOOK IN BOOKS

WHEN THE EMPEROR ERRS
THE PEASANT SHIVERS

TO KNOW THE ROAD AHEAD
ASK THOSE COMING BACK

SCHOLARS TALK BOOKS
BUTCHERS TALK PIGS

HE WHO RIDES THE CHAIR
IS A MAN...
LIKE THOSE WHO CARRY IT

WATER AND WORDS...
EASY TO POUR
IMPOSSIBLE TO RECOVER

HEAVEN LENT YOU A SOUL
EARTH WILL LEND A GRAVE

THE HOUSE WITH AN OLD
GRANDPARENT
HARBORS A JEWEL

THE HEART
OF A LITTLE CHILD...
PURE AS THE BUDDHA

BETTER TO BELIEVE
TOO MUCH
THAN NOTHING AT ALL

BETTER TO BE KIND AT HOME
THAN BURN INCENSE
FAR AWAY

RICHES ADD TO THE HOUSE
VIRTUES TO THE MAN

REFORM A GAMBLER ...
CURE LEPROSY

TOO MUCH TALK
BEWARE TROUBLE ...
TOO MUCH FOOD
BEWARE INDIGESTION

WHEN THE MELON RIPENS
IT WILL FALL OF ITSELF

TAKE A SECOND LOOK ...
IT COSTS YOU NOTHING

FROG IN A DEEP WELL ...
HAPPY FROG

GOLD HAS ITS PRICE
LEARNING IS BEYOND PRICE

EASY TO BEND THE BODY...
NOT THE WILL

ENOUGH SHOVELS OF EARTH
A MOUNTAIN...
ENOUGH PAILS OF WATER
A RIVER

TO SUCCEED, CONSULT
THREE OLD PEOPLE

IF YOU HURRY
THROUGH LONG DAYS...
YOU WILL HURRY
THROUGH SHORT YEARS

TOUCH BLACK PAINT...
HAVE BLACK FINGERS

DO NOT PRAY FOR GOLD...
PRAY FOR GOOD CHILDREN
HAPPY GRANDCHILDREN

VIRTUE: CLIMBING A HILL
VICE: RUNNING DOWN

WIFE OF ONE ... MAY NOT
EAT THE RICE OF TWO

IF HEAVEN MADE HIM
EARTH CAN FIND SOME USE
FOR HIM

AROUND A WIDOW'S DOOR
GREEN SLANDERS GROW

TO UNDERSTAND
YOUR PARENT'S LOVE
BEAR YOUR OWN CHILDREN

LOOKING FOR FISH?
DON'T CLIMB A TREE

THE OLDER THE GINGER
THE MORE IT BITES

FAR WATERS CANNOT
QUENCH NEAR FIRES

CARELESS RAT CHEWING
ON A CAT'S TAIL . . .
BEWARE LIGHTNING!

THE INNKEEPER . . . ONE HOST
UNWORRIED BY GUESTS'
BIG APPETITES

THE CLEVEREST
DAUGHTER-IN-LAW
CANNOT STEW AN EMPTY POT

YOU WANT NO ONE
TO KNOW IT? . . .
THEN DON'T DO IT

VIRTUE BECOMES A WIFE
BEAUTY BECOMES
A CONCUBINE

SIMPLE TO OPEN A SHOP...
ANOTHER THING
TO KEEP IT OPEN

THE RICH
COUNT YEAR TO YEAR...
THE POOR DAY TO DAY

YOU CANNOT DRAW
WHITE CLOTH
FROM A DYEING VAT

DO NOT OPEN A SHOP
UNLESS YOU LIKE TO SMILE

TODAY'S WINE
I SWALLOW NOW...
TOMORROW'S SORROW
I'LL SWALLOW THEN

DON'T LAUGH AT AGE...
PRAY TO REACH IT TOO

WHAT THE EYE SEES NOT
THE HEART CRAVES NOT

FORTUNE AND FLOWERS
DO NOT LAST FOREVER

MORE THAN ONE TREE
GAVE WOOD
TO BUILD THIS TEMPLE

EASY TO BELIEVE
IN HEAVEN'S LAW. . .
BUT SO HARD TO KEEP

THE PEONY IS BEAUTIFUL
YET IT IS SUPPORTED
BY A STALK

WHEN THE MANTIS
HUNTS THE LOCUST. . .
HE FORGETS THE SHRIKE
THAT'S HUNTING HIM

FORGET THE FAVORS
YOU HAVE GIVEN . . .
REMEMBER THOSE RECEIVED

WHO RULES BY CRUELTY
MUST SLEEP LIGHTLY
OR SLEEP LONG

TEACH YOUR SON
AT THE TABLE
YOUR WIFE ON THE PILLOW

IN EVERY FAMILY'S
COOKING-POT. . .
ONE BLACK SPOT

DEAD SONG-BIRDS
MAKE A SAD MEAL

THE TONGUE
A TERRIBLE WEAPON . . .
CRUSHES MEN TO DEATH

THE COURT OFFICIAL
IN ONE LIFE
HAS SEVEN REBIRTHS
AS A BEGGAR

OF A DEAD LEOPARD
WE KEEP THE SKIN . . .
OF MAN HIS REPUTATION

THOUGH MY LEFT HAND
DEFEAT THE RIGHT . . .
WHO WINS?

THE GREAT ELEPHANT . . .
HUNTED FOR IVORY COMBS

LEARNING
IS ROWING UPSTREAM . . .
ADVANCE OR LOSE ALL

PRIESTS RETURN
TO THE TEMPLE
MERCHANTS TO THE SHOP

LONG ROADS TEST THE HORSE
LONG DEALINGS THE FRIEND

WHEN THE TREE FALLS
THE SHADOW FLIES

THE CAREFUL FOOT
CAN WALK ANYWHERE

I DREAMED A THOUSAND
NEW PATHS...
I WOKE AND WALKED
MY OLD ONE

WHEN THE TREE WAVES
WIND IS STIRRING

BETTER FRIENDS VISIT
THAN LIVE WITH YOU

MEN STARE AT THE PROFIT
AND STEP IN THE PITFALL

WINE FLUSHES THE FACE
BUT WEALTH
QUICKENS THE HEART

LEARN TO HANDLE
A WRITING-BRUSH...
AND YOU'LL NEVER HANDLE
A BEGGING-BOWL

OXEN PLOW THE FIELD
BUT HORSES EAT THE GRAIN

IF THE DOG LEAVES
WHEN THE CAT ENTERS...
NO FIGHT TODAY

NO DETERMINATION...
UNTEMPERED STEEL

DON'T ASK THE GUEST
IF YOU SHOULD KILL
YOUR HEN

THOUGH EVIL WHISPERS
HEAVEN HEARS IT
LOUD AS THUNDER

PEACE AND TRANQUILITY...
A THOUSAND GOLD-PIECES

FOLLOW BUSY MEN
AND SLEEP INDOORS . . .
FOLLOW BEGGARS
AND SLEEP OUTDOORS

WE CAN STUDY
UNTIL OLD AGE . . .
AND STILL NOT FINISH

IN BED BE WIFE AND HUSBAND
IN HALL EACH OTHER'S
HONORED GUEST

O EGGS, NEVER FIGHT
WITH STONES!

MEN WHO LIVE TOO NEAR
THE TEMPLE
LAUGH AT THE GODS

STAND OVER WORKMEN
AT THEIR LABORS
NOT THEIR MEALS

IF YOU GIVE NO HELP
TO OTHERS . . .
YOU ARE WASTING
THOSE PRAYERS TO BUDDHA

MANY A GOOD FACE
UNDER A RAGGED HAT

DOGS HAVE NO PREJUDICE
AGAINST THE POOR

IF YOU STAND STRAIGHT
DO NOT FEAR
A CROOKED SHADOW

THREE YEARS TO LEARN
INDUSTRY. . .
THREE DAYS TO LEARN
IDLENESS

WHEN HEAVEN WANTS RAIN
WHEN WIDOWS
WANT REMARRIAGE . . .
IT WILL BE SO

DIVIDE AN ORANGE . . .
IT TASTES JUST AS GOOD

SON WITHOUT LEARNING:
YOU HAVE RAISED AN ASS . . .
DAUGHTER
WITHOUT LEARNING:
YOU HAVE RAISED A PIG

RIVERS AND MOUNTAINS
MAY CHANGE . . .
HUMAN NATURE NEVER

AN INCH OF GOLD
CANNOT PURCHASE
AN INCH OF TIME

JADE AND MEN...
BOTH ARE SHAPED
BY BITTER TOOLS

STUPID IS HAPPY...
HAPPY IS NOT ALWAYS
STUPID

THE MIND...
EMPEROR OF THE BODY

FROM A GABLED ROOF
THE ROLLING MELON
HAS TWO CHOICES

MANY BOOKS
DO NOT USE UP WORDS...
MANY WORDS
DO NOT USE UP THOUGHT

A BAD WORD WHISPERED
WILL ECHO
A HUNDRED MILES

IN LIFE BEWARE THE JUDGE
IN DEATH THE DEVIL

EASY TO ENROLL
A THOUSAND SOLDIERS ...
BUT AH, ONE GENERAL!

IN THE THEATER
FREE SEATS HISS FIRST

RUNAWAY SON
A SHINING JEWEL ...
RUNAWAY DAUGHTER
TARNISHED

BEAT YOUR DRUM
INSIDE THE HOUSE
TO SPARE THE NEIGHBORS

WATER FLOATS A SHIP
WATER SINKS A SHIP

WHAT DO FINE HORSEMEN
KNOW OF ACHING FEET?

A LITTLE IMPATIENCE...
BIG PLANS RUINED

A WHALE
IN SHALLOW WATER
AMUSES THE SHRIMPS

NEW CLOTHES ARE BEST...
AND OLD FRIENDS

A GOOD TEACHER...
BETTER THAN A BARROWFUL
OF BOOKS

FIRST SEE THE HARE...
THEN LOOSE THE FALCON

THE SAVING MAN
BECOMES THE FREE MAN

YOU BURN INCENSE
BEFORE THE GOD...
AND THEN TOPPLE HIM

YOU CANNOT HOOK TROUT?
TRY DIGGING CLAMS

THE BEST MEMORY...
NOT SO FIRM
AS FADED INK

CLIMB MOUNTAINS
TO SEE LOWLANDS

LEARNING IS WEIGHTLESS...
TREASURE YOU ALWAYS
CARRY EASILY

CUSTOMERS ARE JADE
MERCHANDISE IS GRASS

LAWS CONTROL
THE LESSER MAN...
RIGHT CONDUCT CONTROLS
THE GREATER ONE

EASIER TO RULE A NATION
THAN A SON

THE MESSENGER OF DEATH
ENTERS...
AND ALL BUSINESS STOPS

INSECTS DO NOT NEST
IN A BUSY DOOR-HINGE

UNPLOWED FIELDS MAKE
HOLLOW BELLIES...
UNREAD BOOKS MAKE
HOLLOW MINDS

BIGGEST PROFITS
MEAN GRAVEST RISKS

DISEASES ARE OFTEN CURED
NEVER FATE

WHILE YOU ARE BARGAINING
CONCEAL YOUR COIN

LEARNING IS TREASURE
NO THIEF CAN TOUCH

TO STOP DRINKING...
STUDY A DRUNKARD
WHILE YOU ARE SOBER

SORROW IS THE CHILD
OF TOO MUCH JOY

WITH MONEY A DRAGON
WITHOUT MONEY A WORM

AT THE BATHING BEACH
WHICH MEN
ARE GENTLEMEN?

UGLY WIVES
STUPID SERVANT GIRLS ...
WHAT TREASURES!

SPRING ... CHANGEABLE
AS STEPMOTHER'S FACE

WITHOUT SORROWS
NO ONE BECOMES A SAINT

AT BIRTH WE COME
AT DEATH WE GO ...
BEARING NOTHING

O MAN, YOU WHO DO NOT
LIVE A HUNDRED ...
WHY FRET A THOUSAND?

MAN HAS
A THOUSAND PLANS ...
HEAVEN BUT ONE

HEAVEN IS ONLY THREE FEET
ABOVE YOUR HEAD

SOFT GRASS
FOLLOWS EVERY BREEZE

DO NOT PEDDLE WOOD
IN THE FOREST. . .
OR FISH BY THE LAKE SHORE

HAPPY PEOPLE
NEVER COUNT
HOURS AS THEY PASS

AN OLD FRIEND MET
IN A FAR COUNTRY. . .
RAIN AFTER DROUGHT

THE PINE STAYS GREEN
IN WINTER . . .
WISDOM IN HARDSHIP

NO SHADE-TREE?
BLAME NOT THE SUN
BUT YOURSELF

THREE FEET OF ICE . . .
NOT FROZEN IN ONE DAY

WITH VIRTUE YOU CANNOT
BE ENTIRELY POOR . . .
WITHOUT IT YOU CANNOT
BE REALLY RICH

IF THE OX WON'T DRINK
DON'T TRY TO BEND HIS NECK

GREAT DOUBTS
DEEP WISDOM . . .
SMALL DOUBTS
LITTLE WISDOM

TO LOCK UP MISCHIEF
SHUT YOUR MOUTH

WHEN THE WATERS SINK
THE STONES SHOW

IF THE FIRST WORDS FAIL . . .
TEN THOUSAND
WILL NOT THEN AVAIL

WHEN THE EMPEROR GLARES
THAT MAN IS DEAD

MANKIND FEARS AN EVIL MAN
BUT HEAVEN DOES NOT . . .

MANKIND SCORNS
A VIRTUOUS MAN
BUT HEAVEN DOES NOT

TO LIGHT THE LAMP
BEFORE BUDDHA . . .
FIRST EXTINGUISH SELF

BETTER DIE TEN YEARS EARLY
THAN LIVE TEN YEARS POOR

POOR IN TROUBLES . . .
POOR IN DREAMS

BUTTERFLIES
SHOULD NOT TALK OF SNOW
NOR WORMS OF HEAVEN

DEER-HUNTER . . .
WASTE NOT YOUR ARROW
ON THE HARE

TO HAVE PRINCIPLES
FIRST HAVE COURAGE

THE WISE MAN
HEARKENS TO HIS MIND . . .
THE FOOLISH MAN
TO HIS CRONIES

IF IN THE DARK
HE KNEELS TO PRAY . . .
HE REALLY PRAYS

TOWERS ARE MEASURED
BY THEIR SHADOWS...
GREAT MEN BY THOSE
WHO SPEAK ILL OF THEM

ONE LAMP CANNOT LIGHT
TWO HOUSES

MAN'S LIFE...
CANDLE IN THE WIND
FROST ON THE TILES

WINE IN SMALL GULPS...
KNOWLEDGE IN LARGE

THE HAPPINESS
IN YOUR POCKET...
DON'T SPEND IT ALL

IN PRESENCE OF PRINCES
THE CLEVEREST JESTER
IS MUTE

HEAT COMES EQUALLY
TO ALL...
COLD RESPECTS
THE RICH MAN'S FURS

GOOD DEEDS STAY INDOORS...
EVIL DEEDS TRAVEL
MANY MILES FROM HOME

WHEN THE THATCH IS THIN:
THUNDERSTORMS...
WHEN THE JUNK SETS SAIL:
HEADWINDS

TILE TOSSED
OVER THE WALL...
WHO CAN TELL
WHERE IT MAY FALL?

MEN KNOW NOT ALL
THEIR FAULTS...
OXEN ALL THEIR STRENGTH

A WHITEWASHED CROW
SOON SHOWS BLACK AGAIN

MEN FATED TO BE HAPPY
NEED NOT HASTE

IF YOU ALWAYS GIVE
YOU WILL ALWAYS HAVE

WITH MONEY YOU CAN CALL
THE VERY GODS TO HELP...
WITHOUT IT
NOT A SINGLE MAN

BLAME YOURSELF
AS YOU BLAME OTHERS...
FORGIVE OTHERS
AS YOU FORGIVE YOURSELF

ONLY TWO KINDS OF MEN
ARE GOOD...
BURIED AND UNBORN

IN HIS DECISION
THE JUDGE
WITH SEVEN REASONS
GIVES ONLY ONE IN COURT

ONE FAMILY
BUILDS THE WALL...
TWO FAMILIES ENJOY IT

AMONG TEN MATCHMAKERS
ONLY NINE WILL LIE

ONE DAY WITHOUT FOOD
A HUSBAND TURNS COLD...
THREE DAYS WITHOUT FOOD
A WIFE TURNS COLD

TRAVELING BY BOAT?
PREPARE FOR WETTING

TEACHERS OPEN THE DOOR...
YOU ENTER BY YOURSELF

THOUSAND YEARS A GHOST...
AH, BETTER ONE DAY A MAN

TOO OFTEN
GREAT POLITENESS MEANS:
I WANT SOMETHING

HE USES CANNON
TO SHOOT BIRDS

KNOW THYSELF
TO KNOW OTHERS...
FOR HEART
BEATS LIKE HEART

LEAVE A BIT OF THE TAIL
TO WHISK OFF FLIES

PICK YOUR INN
BEFORE THE DARK...
GET ON YOUR ROAD
BEFORE THE DAWN

IN THE LITTLE BOY
SEE THE FINAL MAN

NINE SONS SHE BORE . . .
NINE SEPARATE CHARACTERS

HIS VIRTUES EXCEED
HIS TALENTS . . .
A SUPERIOR MAN

HIS TALENTS EXCEED
HIS VIRTUES . . .
AN INFERIOR ONE

SOFT TONGUE STAYS . . .
HARD TEETH FALL

ONE RAT-DROPPING
SPOILS A POT OF RICE

SILLY TOAD: PLANNING
A MEAL OF GOOSE!

WHILE YOU HOLD THE BOW
IN PAWN...
YOU ARE SAFE FROM ARROWS

A BIG FISH...
THE ONE THAT GOT AWAY

PLAN YOUR YEAR IN SPRING
YOUR DAY AT DAWN

THE TONGUE LIKE A
SHARP KNIFE... KILLS
WITHOUT DRAWING BLOOD

WHEN YOU GO OUT
WATCH THE CLOUDY SKY...
WHEN YOU GO IN
WATCH YOUR HOST'S EYE

WHEN BROTHERS SPLIT...
OUTSIDERS
ENTER THE BREACH

TWO BARRELS OF TEARS
DO NOT HEAL A BRUISE

PRACTICE NO VICE
BECAUSE IT'S TRIVIAL...
NEGLECT NO VIRTUE
BECAUSE IT'S SO

NURTURE THE PLANT
ONE YEAR...
TEN DAYS OF FLOWERS

FRIENDSHIP OF OFFICIALS...
THIN AS THEIR PAPERS

'TWIXT MONASTERY
AND CONVENT
NO INTERCOURSE...
THEY SAY

ATTEND THE EMPEROR...
SLEEP WITH A TIGER

RICH MEN
ACCUMULATE MONEY...
POOR ACCUMULATE YEARS

THE WISE MAN TARRIES NOT
TO INSTRUCT THE FOOL

LIFE IS A DREAM WALKING
DEATH IS A GOING HOME

EASIER TO BEND
THE BODY THAN THE MIND

STOUT MEN
NOT STOUT WALLS
MAKE THE STOUT CITY

FATHER: NEVER GO BOND
FOR A DAUGHTER'S VIRTUE

ENTIRE LEISURE FOR A DAY...
IMMORTALITY IN LITTLE

TO BE HEARD AFAR...
BANG YOUR GONG
ON A HILL-TOP

MAN CONCOCTS
A MILLION SCHEMES...
GOD KNOWS BUT ONE

RICHES: A DREAM
IN THE NIGHT...
FAME: A GULL
FLOATING ON WATER

YOU CAN'T CLAP
WITH ONE HAND ONLY

MY TEACHER FOR ONE DAY
MY FATHER FOR LIFE

WITHOUT DETERMINATION
MAN IS AN
UNTEMPERED SWORD

SILLY BOYS
IN TIME BECOME
SILLY OLD MEN

PURE GOLD DOES NOT FEAR
THE SMELTER

FIRST HALF THE NIGHT
THINK OF
YOUR OWN FAULTS . . .
SECOND HALF
THE FAULTS OF OTHERS

NO MEDICINES CAN CURE
THE VULGAR MAN

THE EMPEROR IS RICH
BUT HE CANNOT BUY
ONE EXTRA YEAR

BROTHERS
ARE LIKE HANDS AND FEET

THE BEST HORSE
CANNOT WEAR TWO SADDLES

IF YOUR SONS ARE GOOD
DO YOU NEED MONEY?
IF YOUR SONS ARE BAD
SHOULD YOU KEEP MONEY?

NO ROAD TO HAPPINESS
OR SORROW...
FIND THEM IN YOURSELF

THREE EARLY RISINGS
MAKE AN EXTRA DAY

MONEY COMES LIKE SAND
SCOOPED WITH A NEEDLE...
MONEY GOES LIKE SAND
WASHED BY WATER

A BEAUTIFUL BIRD...
THE ONLY KIND WE CAGE

DELICACY OF THE FEAST...
THE LEARNED GUEST

MAN CANNOT STIR ONE INCH
WITHOUT THE PUSH
OF HEAVEN'S FINGER

MISTRESS SLACK
SERVANTS SLOVEN

DON'T WASTE YOUR HOUR:
THE SUN SETS SOON

LIGHTS OF A
THOUSAND STARS
DO NOT MAKE ONE MOON

NO GUESTS AT HOME...
NO HOSTS ABROAD

DON'T USE OILED PAPER
TO WRAP UP FIRE

BLIND LEADING THE BLIND...
BEWARE THE RIVER EDGE!

GREAT BUSINESS IS GOOD...
TO SIT AND SIP THIS GLASS
IS BETTER

GET THE COFFIN READY...
WATCH THE MAN MEND

SLOW WORK ... FINE WORK

WHEN GUESTS HAVE GONE
THE HOST BREATHES DEEP

NOT WINE ... MEN
INTOXICATE THEMSELVES;
NOT VICE ... MEN
ENTICE THEMSELVES

CHEAT THE EARTH...
EARTH WILL CHEAT YOU

"I HEARD" IS GOOD...
"I SAW" IS BETTER

THE PEN CAN KILL A MAN...
NO KNIFE IS NEEDED

HE COMES WITH INCENSE
IN ONE HAND...
IN THE OTHER A SPEAR

WHEN THE CAT IS GONE...
THE MICE
COME OUT TO STRETCH

BLESSINGS NEVER COME
IN PAIRS...
ILLS NEVER COME ALONE

THOUGH A TREE GROW
A THOUSAND FEET...
THE FRUITS WILL FALL
TO EARTH AGAIN